CEREMONIES

CEREMONIES

PHOTOGRAPHS BY PETER MAGUBANE

TEXT BY SANDRA KLOPPER

Published by Struik Publishers
(a division of New Holland Publishing (South Africa) (Pty) Ltd)

London • Cape Town • Sydney • Auckland

Garfield House   14 Aquatic Drive
86 Edgware Road   Frenchs Forest
W2 2EA London   NSW 2086
United Kingdom   Australia

80 McKenzie Street   218 Lake Road
Cape Town 8001   Northcote, Auckland
South Africa   New Zealand

Website: **www.struik.co.za**

ISBN 1 86872 515 4

Design director   Janice Evans
Publishing manager   Annlerie van Rooyen
Design   Illana Fridkin
Managing editor   Lesley Hay-Whitton
Proofreader   Glynne Newlands
French translator   Jean-Paul Houssière
German translator   Friedel Herrmann

10 9 8 7 6 5 4 3 2 1

Reproduction by Hirt & Carter (Cape) Pty Ltd
Printed and bound by APP Printers, Singapore

Front cover: Xhosa initiates.
Back cover: Bantwane novice diviners at their
initiation ceremony.
Page 1: Ndebele initiate on his return home.
Page 2 (left): Xhosa initiate.
Page 2 (right): Zulu u*memulo* (coming-of-age) ceremony.
Page 3 (left): South Sotho female initiates.
Page 3 (right): Batlhaping initiates on their return home.
Opposite: Bantwane married women.
Page 6: Already initiated Bantwane girls attending the
coming-out ceremony of younger female initiates.

INTRODUCTION

Across the world, communities mark major transitions in life through celebrations and ceremonies. From birth to death, these rites of passage regulate and give expression to meaningful changes in people's lives. They also play a role in drawing attention both to the individual's emergence from childhood and the assumption of responsibilities associated with the transition to adult life. In South Africa, many ceremonies and celebrations are also aimed, more specifically, at securing the spiritual well-being, not only of the individual, but also of the community as a whole. Throughout the region, this aim is achieved above all by appeasing and paying homage to the ancestors. Although most ceremonies of this kind are generally conducted by the male heads of households, the ancestors usually communicate their desires and concerns to their descendants through the mediation of ritual specialists commonly known as *izangoma*.

Until the late 18th century all chiefdoms in southern Africa observed initiation practices to prepare young people for their roles in adult society. In present-day KwaZulu-Natal, these rites were abandoned in favour of age-grade regiments over a generation before the rise to power, in the early 19th century, of the first Zulu king, Shaka. A number of celebrations associated with the coming of age of young women nevertheless survive to this day, while the Reed Ceremony, associated with puberty rites among the Swazi, was adopted by their Zulu-speaking neighbours as late as the mid-1980s.

Among other southern African groups there was a revival of interest in initiation rites in the course of the 1990s. In keeping with this trend, young people from urban areas often participate in ceremonies organized by rural chiefs and ritual specialists. Partly for this reason, it has become increasingly common for these ceremonies to include participants from diverse ethnic backgrounds. From time to time, initiation schools also attract the offspring of families who now live abroad. Since male circumcision practices are delayed until men are in their late teens or early twenties among groups like the Tswana, Sotho, Xhosa and Ndebele, it is especially these ceremonies that are attracting increasing numbers of outsiders. In contrast to this, initiation tends to coincide with the transition to puberty among groups like the Pedi and Bantwane.

INTRODUCTION

Les peuples du monde célèbrent fréquemment les diverses transitions d'un stade de la vie vers l'autre par des fêtes et des cérémonies. Du moment de la naissance jusqu'à la mort, les rites de passage ordonnent ces transitions et permettent aux gens de trouver un sens à la vie. C'est en partie pour cette raison que les rites sont souvent importants, attirant l'attention sur l'individu qui sort de l'enfance, et sa prise en charge des responsabilités associées avec le passage vers l'âge adulte. En Afrique du Sud, de nombreuses cérémonies ont pour but de mener au bien-être spirituel, non seulement des individus, mais également de la communauté en général. Partout dans le pays, ce but est atteint principalement en apaisant les ancêtres et en leur rendant hommage. Bien que la plupart des cérémonies de ce genre soient généralement présidées par les chefs de familles, normalement les ancêtres communiquent leurs désirs et préoccupations à leurs descendants par l'intermédiaire de spécialistes en matières rituelles, appelés *izangoma*.

Jusqu'à la fin du 18ième toutes les peuplades de l'Afrique australe pratiquaient diverses cérémonies d'initiations préparant les jeunes, hommes et femmes, pour le rôle qu'ils auront à jouer quand ils atteindront l'âge adulte. Toutefois, à la province de KwaZulu-Natal, plus d'une génération avant l'accession au pouvoir au début du 19ième de Chaka, le premier roi des Zoulous, ces rites furent délaissés en faveur de régiments pour jeunes gens d'âge semblable, et venant de régions différentes.

Néanmoins, plusieurs cérémonies dédiées aux jeunes femmes approchant la majorité, survivent à ce jour; d'autre part, les Zoulous, vers le milieu des années 80 adoptèrent de leurs voisins Swazis la 'Reed Ceremony' (cérémonie des roseaux), qui est liée aux rites de la puberté.

Parmi les autres peuples d'Afrique australe, il y eut, au cours des années 90, un regain d'intérêt dans les rites d'initiation pour filles et garçons. En conséquence, on voit souvent des jeunes des secteurs urbains venir participer aux cérémonies rurales organisées par les chefs et spécialistes rituels. C'est une des raisons pour laquelle les participants appartiennent souvent à différents groupes ethniques. De temps en temps, ces écoles d'initiation attirent la progéniture de familles vivant à l'étranger. Puisque les Tswanas, Sothos, Xhosas et Ndebeles ne se font circoncire que vers la fin de l'adolescence ou au début de la vingtaine, ce sont généralement leurs cérémonies qui attirent le plus les étrangers. Par contre, chez les Pedis et Bantwanes, l'initiation coïncide généralement avec l'avènement de la puberté.

EINFÜHRUNG

Weltweit begehen Volksgruppen bedeutsame Lebensstationen durch entsprechende Zeremonien und Feierlichkeiten. Von der Geburt bis zum Tode regulieren und markieren diese Übergangsriten den Wechsel in eine neue Lebensphase. Daher spielen sie oft eine wichtige Rolle im Hinweis darauf, daß die Kindheit nun zurückliegt und daß mit dem Eintritt in das erwachsene Leben entsprechende Verantwortungen übernommen werden müssen. In Südafrika erstrecken sich viele Zeremonien und Feierlichkeiten über den Einzelnen hinaus auf das spirituelle Wohlergehen der Gemeinschaft als Ganzes. Weitverbreitet ist die Gepflogenheit, die Ahnen durch Verehrung und Befriedigung günstig zu stimmen. Obgleich dieserart Zeremonien generell vom männlichen Oberhaupt des Haushalts zelebriert wird, bekunden die Vorfahren ihre Bedürfnisse den Nachfahren gewöhnlich durch die Vermittlung befugter Ritualisten, allgemein als *izangoma* bekannt.

Bis ins späte 18. Jahrhundert befolgten alle Häuptlingstümer im südlichen Afrika Initiationspraktiken, um junge Männer und Frauen auf ihre zukünftige Rolle in der erwachsenen Gesellschaft vorzubereiten. Im heutigen KwaZulu-Natal, jedoch, gab man diese Riten zugunsten von Regimentern in Altersgruppen auf. Dieser Wandel vollzog sich mehr als eine Generation vor dem ersten Zulukönig, Shaka, im frühen 19. Jahrhundert. Einige Feiern im Zusammenhang mit der Volljährigkeit junger Frauen, haben dennoch bis heute überlebt, und die 'Schilfzeremonie', die zu den Pubertätsriten der Swazi gehört, wurde sogar erst so unlängst wie Mitte der achtziger Jahre von den Zulu übernommen.

Volksgruppen im südlichen Afrika zeigten in den 1990er Jahren Wiederbelebungen des Interesses an weiblichen und männlichen Initiationsriten. Dieser Trend bewog junge Leute in städtischen Gebieten dazu, an Feiern teilzunehmen, die ländliche Häuptlinge und Ritualisten organisierten. Vermehrt nehmen Angehörige unterschiedlicher ethnischer Gruppen an diesen Zeremonien teil. Zeitweilig wohnen sogar Kinder von Familien, die jetzt in Übersee leben, diesen Initiationsschulen bei. Da die männliche Beschneidung bei den Tswana, Sotho, Xhosa und Ndebele hinausgezögert wird, bis die jungen Männer in die späten Teenagerjahre oder frühen Zwanziger kommen, zieht gerade dieser Brauch eine wachsende Anzahl Auswärtiger an. Die Pedi und Bantwane, wiederum, halten Initiationsriten bei Pubertätseintritt ab.

Initiation ceremonies associated with girls among the Bantwane from Mpumalanga province include mock circumcision practices. These rites of passage, however, are aimed primarily at preparing women for their future roles as wives and mothers. As such, initiation practices generally stress the importance of appropriate social and sexual behaviour in adult life.

Parmi les Bantwanes de la province de Mpumalanga, l'initiation des jeunes filles comprend des simulations de la circoncision, bien que ces rites de passage soient principalement destinés à préparer les jeunes femmes pour leurs futurs rôles d'épouses et de mères. A proprement parler, l'initiation met principalement l'accent sur l'importance d'un comportement adulte correct, tant en matière sociale que sexuelle.

Bei den Bantwane in Mpumalanga ist eine angedeutete Beschneidung Teil der Initiationspraktiken bei jungen Mädchen. Die ‚Riten des Übergangs' zielen jedoch vornehmlich darauf ab, Mädchen auf ihre zukünftige Rolle als Ehefrau und Mutter vorzubereiten, und bei den Einführungskursen wird vorrangig die Bedeutung des angemessenen sozialen und sexuellen Verhaltens im Erwachsenenleben betont.

All male and female initiation rites involve the adoption of hairstyles and clothing that underline the transitional status of the initiates. Preparing young women for their roles as wives and mothers, Bantwane female initiates shave their heads in emulation of the 'bicycle seat' hairstyles associated with mature women.

L'initiation tant des filles que des garçons, exige que coiffures et accoutrements soulignent la situation transitoire des initiés. En prévision de leurs rôles d'épouses et de mères, les jeunes initiées bantwanes se rasent la tête dans le style 'selle de bicyclette' comparable à celui des femmes adultes.

Bei allen Initiationssriten, männlichen und weiblichen, spielen besondere Frisuren und Kleidung eine wichtige Rolle, um den Übergangsstatus der Teilnehmer zu betonen. Um auf ihre zukünftige Rolle als Frau und Mutter hinzuweisen, rasieren sich bei den Bantwane die weiblichen Initianden den Kopf, in Anlehnung an die ‚Fahrradsattel-Frisur' der reifen Frau.

Female Pedi initiates wear a short, stringed front apron and leather back apron but their torsos remain uncovered throughout the iniation process. It is only once women have children that they are required to cover their breasts to signify their status as mature, married women.

Les initiées pedis portent un petit tablier en corde devant, et en cuir à l'arrière, et leur torse restera à découvert durant toute la période d'initiation. Par contre, une fois que ces femmes auront un enfant, elles seront tenues de se couvrir les seins pour marquer leur statut de femme adulte et mariée.

Weibliche Initiandinnen der Pedi tragen knappe Schurze, vorn aus Schnüren und hinten aus Leder, aber der Oberkörper bleibt unverhüllt. Erst, wenn eine Frau Kinder geboren hat, wird erwartet, daß sie ihre Brüste bedeckt, um ihre Stellung als reife, verheiratete Frau zu bekunden.

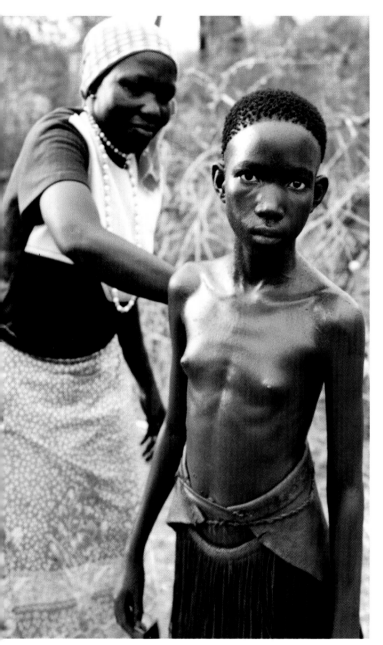

In common with initiates in other parts of South Africa, the bodies of Pedi girls are rubbed with fat and ochre, and charcoal and other substances are smeared into their hair. In recognition of their child-bearing potential, they are adorned with grass ornaments, associated with fertility, and often receive gifts like sweets on their return to the community.

Comme les autres initiées en Afrique du Sud, la peau des jeunes pedis est badigeonnée de suif et d'ocre; du charbon de bois et autres substances sont aussi enduits dans leur chevelure. Pour marquer leur nubilité, elles sont parées d'ornements fait d'herbes symbolisant la fécondité; souvent aussi, on leur offre des douceurs quand elles rejoignent leur communauté.

Wie auch bei anderen Volksgruppen in Südafrika wird der Körper der Pedi-Mädchen mit Fett und Ocker eingerieben, und die Haare werden unter anderem mit Kohle eingeschmiert. Da sie jetzt im gebärfähigen Alter sind, wird ihnen Grasschmuck angelegt, ein symbolischer Hinweis auf Fruchtbarkeit, und sie erhalten bei ihrer Rückkehr in die Gemeinschaft oft Geschenke, etwa Süßigkeiten.

Although they attend different initiation lodges, both male and female initiates on their return to the community wear large quantities of beadwork, which is usually made by their mothers. When participants from many communities are involved in initiation, long-standing cultural interactions between neighbouring groups like the Pedi and the Bantwane may be seen in the styles of the beadwork.

Bien que filles et garçons n'aillent pas aux mêmes écoles d'initiation, au retour dans leur communauté, tous portent de nombreux ornements fait de perles, normalement fait par leur mère. Lorsque les membres de nombreuses communautés différentes participent à l'initiation, l'interaction culturelle entre groupes voisins comme les Pedis et les Bantwanes peut se voir dans le style des ornements.

Obwohl die Initiationslager nach Geschlechtern getrennt abgehalten werden, tragen weibliche wie auch männliche Teilnehmer bei ihrer Rückkehr in die Gemeinschaft viel Perlenschmuck, der meist von den Müttern angefertigt wurde. Wenn Initianden aus unterschiedlichen Volksgruppen am Kurs teilgenommen haben, kann man am Perlenschmuck langfristige gegenseitige Beeinflussung unter benachbarten Gruppen, wie etwa den Bantwane und Pedi, ablesen.

It is common for initiates, including Bantwane boys (*see* pages 20-21), to cast their eyes down as a mark of deference. Like initiates elsewhere, Pedi boys are overseen by an initiation master (*right*), who plays a crucial role in these rites of passage. He is responsible for educating and disciplining the initiates.

Il est normal pour les initiés, y compris les garçons bantwanes (*voir* pages 21-22), de baisser les yeux par déférence. Comme ailleurs, les jeunes initiés pedis sont supervisés par un maître (*à droite*), qui joue un rôle vital dans ces rites de passage. Le maître est responsable pour l'éducation et la discipline des initiés.

Es ist üblich, daß Initianden, wie diese Bantwane Knaben (*siehe* Seite 20-21) den Blick ehrerbietig gesenkt halten. Wie andere Initianden unterstehen Pedi Knaben einem Kursleiter (*rechts*), der eine entscheidende Rolle bei den ‚Riten des Übergangs' spielt. Er trägt die Verantwortung für die Schulung und Züchtigung der Teilnehmer.

Sticks play an important symbolic role in male initiation rites. They may be used to teach the boys stick fighting skills and, in the case of older initiates, to mark their transition to manhood. Young boys must conform to the demands of the initiation master, who is usually also responsible for circumcising them.

Les bâtons sont un important symbole dans les rites initiatiques des garçons. Ils peuvent être utilisés pour enseigner l'art du combat aux plus jeunes, et dans le cas des initiés plus âgés, pour indiquer leur avènement à l'âge adulte. Les jeunes garçons doivent se soumettre aux exigences du maître, qui normalement est celui qui les circoncira.

Stöcke haben eine bedeutsame Symbolik bei den Mannbarkeitsriten. Sie dienen dazu, den Knaben Geschicklichkeit bei Stockkämpfen beizubringen, und bei den älteren Teilnehmern kennzeichnen sie deren Übergang ins Mannesalter. Die Knaben müssen die Anordnungen des Kursleiters befolgen, der gewöhnlich auch die Beschneidung bei ihnen vornimmt.

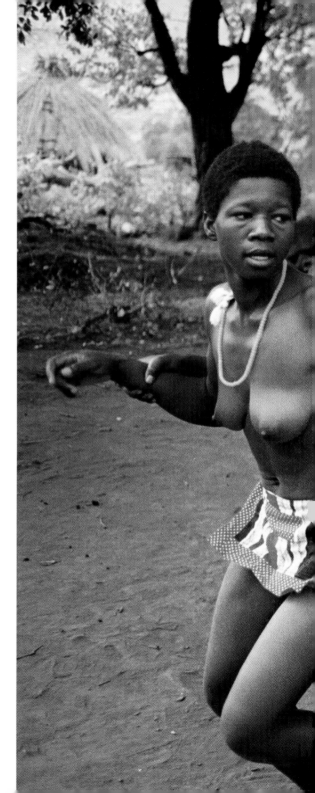

Many young Venda women still attend the *dombani*, a pre-marital school in which participants perform a dance emulating the movement of a python. According to Venda traditionalists, this is associated with fertility.

De nombreuses jeunes Vendas vont toujours au *dombani*, une école où l'on va avant de se marier. Elles y font une danse qui imite les mouvements du python, et qui, selon les traditionalistes Venda, représente la fécondité.

Viele junge Venda-Frauen absolvieren noch die *dombani*, eine Eheschule, wo sie einen Tanz aufführen, der die Bewegungen der Pythonschlange nachahmt. Laut Überlieferung besteht darin ein Zusammenhang mit Fruchtbarkeit.

South Sotho female initiates cover their faces with woven grass masks and wear bulky grass belts associated with fertility. They also decorate their clay-covered bodies with patterns, many of which echo the murals married women paint on their homesteads.

Les initiées south sothos portent des masques et des ceintures en herbes tressées, symbolisant la fécondité. Leur corps qui est recouvert d'argile, est décoré de motifs semblables à ceux que les femmes mariées peignent sur les murs de leurs maisons.

Weibliche Initianden der Süd-Sotho bedecken die Gesichter mit Grasmasken und legen schwere Grasgürtel an, die mit Fruchtbarkeit in Verbindung gebracht werden. Die Muster auf ihren lehmbeschmierten Körpern ähneln den Wandbemalungen auf den Heimstätten.

One of the most important functions of female initiation ceremonies is to underline the need for co-operation and a sense of responsibility to the community. Most South Sotho female initiates are in their late teens or early twenties.

Une des plus importantes fonctions des cérémonies pour jeunes filles, est de renforcer la notion de coopération et de responsabilité vis-à-vis de la communauté. Les initiées south sothos sont souvent à la fin de l'adolescence ou au commencement de la vingtaine.

Eine der wichtigsten Funktionen der Einführung ins Frauenleben liegt in der Betonung auf Zusammenarbeit und Verantwortung der Gemeinschaft gegenüber. Bei den Süd-Sotho sind die meisten weiblichen Teilnehmer im späten Teenageralter oder Anfang Zwanzig.

Initiates' clothing is generally burnt as they leave the initiation lodge. On their return to the community, they are welcomed with gifts. This reunion may be extremely emotional for initiates, who often endure hardship and depravation during their initiation.

A la fin de l'initiation, les vêtements des initiés sont brûlés, et, à leur retour dans la communauté, ils sont accueillis avec des présents. Cette réunion pourra être chargée d'émotions pour les jeunes qui ont souvent enduré beaucoup de souffrances et de privations.

Nach Ablauf der Initiation werden Unterkünfte und Kleidung der Teilnehmer verbrannt. Zur Rückkehr in die Gemeinschaft werden sie mit Geschenken begrüßt. Das Wiedersehen ist oft emotional, denn in der Einführungszeit gab es Entbehrungen und Erniedrigungen.

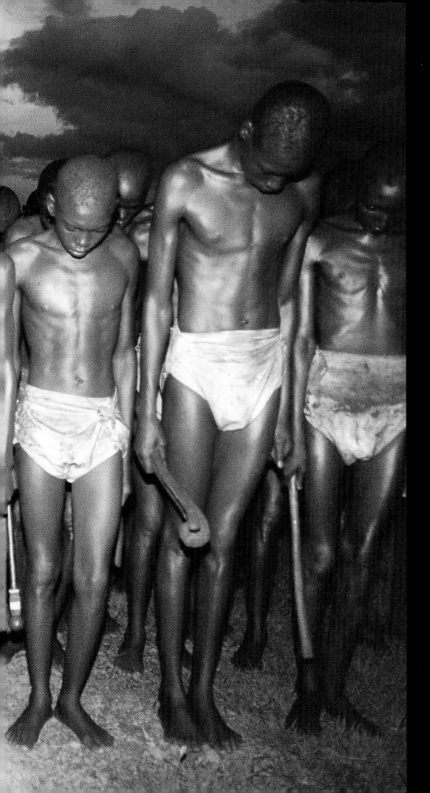

Initiation schools generally lay great emphasis on showing deference to others, especially older people, in part by lowering the head in their presence. But young initiates, like these Sotho youths from the Sasolburg area, are also encouraged to affirm their new status as adult men. For this reason, they all receive fighting sticks as a symbol of their virility.

Les écoles d'initiation insistent que l'on montre grand respect envers autrui, spécialement les anciens, devant qui on baisse la tête. Mais les jeunes initiés, comme ces Sothos de la région de Sasolburg, sont aussi encouragés à manifester leur nouvelle condition d'homme adulte. Pour ce faire, ils reçoivent tous un bâton de combat comme symbole de leur virilité.

In den Einführungskursen wird Achtung anderen – insbesondere älteren – gegenüber stark betont. Das Neigen des Kopfes in deren Gegenwart gilt als respektvolle Haltung. Aber die Initianden, wie diese Sotho-Jünglinge aus der Gegend bei Sasolburg, werden auch ermutigt, den neuerlangten Status als erwachsene Männer zu demonstrieren. Daher erhalten alle einen Kampfstock, Symbol der Virilität.

During the initiation period, young men from most southern African groups receive instruction in the martial art of stick fighting. Once they return to their homes, these sticks are supposed to remain with them for the rest of their lives. Historically adult men carried fighting sticks both to protect themselves and their families from danger, and to hunt small game and birds on their journeys to and from home.

Les jeunes gens de la plupart des peuples d'Afrique australe apprennent l'art du combat au bâton. Une fois retournés chez eux, ces bâtons resteront en leur possession jusqu'à la mort. Traditionnellement, les hommes adultes portent leur bâton pour leur protection et celle de leur famille; ils s'en servent aussi pour chasser le petit gibier lors de leurs déplacements.

Während des Mannbarkeitskurses erhalten die jungen Männer bei den meisten Völkern des südlichen Afrika Unterricht im Stockkämpfen. Wieder heimgekehrt, sollten sie diese Stöcke ihr Leben lang behalten. Traditionsgemäß trugen erwachsene Männer ihre Kampfstöcke, um sich und ihre Familien zu verteidigen – und auch, um unterwegs Vögel und Kleinwild erlegen zu können.

South Sotho initiates receive gifts at their coming-out ceremonies that include beadwork and colourful scarves. They wear dark glasses, not only to signal their status as adults, but also to underline their respect for others by avoiding direct eye contact.

Les South Sothos reçoivent des perles et des foulards à la fin de leur initiation. Ils portent des lunettes noires, non seulement pour indiquer leur condition d'adulte, mais pour éviter ainsi de croiser les autres du regard, ce qui serait manquer de respect.

Initianden der Süd-Sotho erhalten Geschenke zur Abschlußfeier, oft Perlenschmuck und bunte Tücher. Die dunklen Brillen betonen nicht nur ihr Erwachsensein, sondern bekunden auch Achtung anderen gegenüber, indem direkter Augenkontakt vermieden wird.

The beadwork given to South Sotho initiates at coming-out ceremonies often includes items made from small glass beads. But it has become common for beaded garments to be made from larger plastic beads, partly because this is both quicker and cheaper.

Les ornements donnés au jeunes south sothos à la fin de leur initiation sont souvent fait de petites perles de verre. Il devient cependant de plus en plus courant d'utiliser de plus grosses perles de plastique, car la fabrication est plus rapide et moins chère.

Der Perlenschmuck, den Initianden der Süd-Sotho zur Abschlußfeier erhalten, wird meist aus kleinen Glasperlen angefertigt. Aber es hat sich eingebürgert, für Kleidungsstücke größere Plastikperlen zu verwenden, da es preiswerter ist und rascher vonstatten geht.

At their coming-out ceremonies South Sotho initiates recite the praises of their ancestors, highlighting the continuity between the past and the present celebrated in the initiation lodge. Some become openly emotional when they pay homage to their forebears.

Lors des cérémonies finales, les South Sothos rendent hommage à leurs ancêtres, renforçant les liens entre le passé et le présent, comme célébré durant l'initiation. Certains d'entre eux ne cachent pas leurs émotions durant ces moments solennels.

Bei der Abschlußfeier deklamieren Initianden der Süd-Sotho Lobpreisungen auf ihre Ahnen, um – wie schon im Initiationskurs – die Kontinuität zwischen Vergangenheit und Gegenwart zu betonen. Dabei werden manche öffentlich von Gefühlen übermannt.

Ndebele youths wear specific forms of dress at various stages in their rite of passage into adulthood, their clothing marking symbolic moments in the journey between the carefree world of the past and the responsibilities they must embrace in the future.

Les jeunes ndebeles changent d'accoutrements selon le stade atteint dans les rites de passage. Les différents costumes représentent les étapes franchies dans leur périple entre la vie insouciante du passé et les responsabilités qui les attendent dans le futur.

Jugendliche der Ndebele tragen in jeder Phase ihres Heranwachsens bestimmte Kleidungsstücke zur Markierung symbolischer Momente ihrer Wanderung, die sie von der sorgenfreien Welt der Vergangenheit zu den Verantwortungen der Zukunft führt.

Chief Sam Mankoroane (*below*) has been instrumental in reviving initiation rites among the Batlhaping, a sub-section of the Tswana nation: recently over 2,600 youths and almost 800 young women attended his initiation schools.

Le chef Sam Mankoroane (*ci-dessous*) a été pour beaucoup dans le renouveau des rites d'initiation parmi les Batlhapings, un groupe apparenté aux Tswanas. Plus de 2,600 garçons et près de 800 filles ont récemment participé à ses écoles d'initiation.

Häuptling Mankoroane (*unten*) hat maßgeblich ein Aufleben der Initiationsriten unter den Batlhaping, einer Volksgruppe der Tswana, betrieben: unlängst haben etwa 2,600 männliche und nahezu 800 weibliche Jugendliche seine Kurse besucht.

Youths of the Batlhaping group of the Tswana nation wear colourful blankets and beads at their coming-out ceremonies. Like initiates from other parts of the country, they shave their heads when they first enter the initiation school as a symbol of their transitional status, and carry sticks as a symbol of their new status as adults on their return to the community.

Les jeunes gens batlhapings, un groupe apparenté aux Tswanas, portent des couvertures aux couleurs vives et des ornements de perles pour les cérémonies finales. Comme les autres initiés du pays, ils ont la tête rase en symbole de leur condition transitoire lors de l'entrée à l'école d'initiation; et à leur retour dans la communauté, ils portent le bâton symbolisant leur condition d'adulte.

Die jungen Batlhaping, eine Volks-gruppe der Tswana, tragen farben-freudige Decken und Perlenschmuck zu ihren Abschlußfeiern. Wie Initianden aus anderen Gebieten rasieren sie sich zum Kursanfang das Kopfhaar ab, um ihre Über-gangsstellung zu symbolisieren, und wenn sie dann wieder in die Gemeinschaft zurückkehren, tragen sie Stöcke, um ihren neuen Rang als Erwachsene zu demonstrieren.

While the initiation period is characterised by a wealth of activities, youths generally languish in pain in the days immediately after they have been circumcised. Initiates often use cleft sticks to prevent external pressure from aggravating their wounds.

Alors que la période d'initiation est marquée par de nombreuses activités, les jeunes souffrent dans les jours qui suivent leur circoncision. Ils utilisent souvent un bâton fourchu pour éviter toute pression sur leurs plaies.

Obgleich die Zeit der Einführung von viel Aktivität gekennzeichnet ist, winden sich die Knaben in den ersten Tagen nach der Beschneidung vor Schmerzen. Die Teilnehmer benutzen oft gespaltene Stöcke, um äußerlichen Druck von den Wunden abzuhalten.

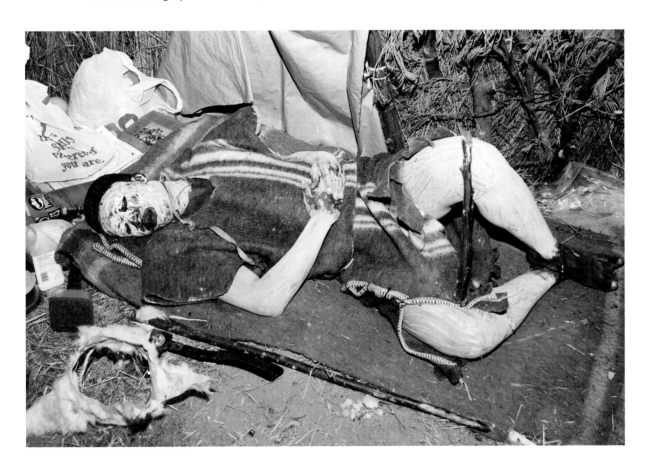

Xhosa initiates build temporary dwellings and make hats from ephemeral materials. Their transitional status is underlined by the wearing of blankets and other makeshift garments during this period in which they denounce contact with the outside world.

Les initiés xhosas construisent des habitations provisoires et fabriquent des couvre-chefs en matériaux précaires. Le port de la couverture et autres vêtements improvisés, indique leur position transitoire durant cette période où ils s'interdisent tout contact avec le monde extérieur.

Initianden der Xhosa bauen Behelfsunterkünfte und fertigen Hüte aus flimsigem Material an. Um den Übergangszustand zu betonen, tragen sie nur Decken und anderen Kleider-ersatz, womit die unterbrochene Verbindung mit der Außenwelt zu veranschault wird.

Like initiates elsewhere who smear themselves with substances like fat or ochre at various stages in their rite of passage into adulthood, Xhosa youths cover their bodies with white clay. This signifies the protection the ancestors afford them during this period.

Ainsi que d'autres initiés qui s'enduisent de substances comme du suif et de l'ocre à divers stades de leur rites de passages vers l'âge adulte, les Xhosas, eux, se recouvrent d'argile. Ceci indique la protection que leur donne les ancêtres durant cette période.

Während sich andere Initianden zu bestimmten Phasen der ‚Riten des Übergangs' mit Fett oder Ocker einreiben, bedecken die Xhosa-Jungen ihre Körper mit weißem Lehm. Dies deutet darauf hin, daß sie in dieser Zeit unter dem Schutz der Ahnen stehen.

Most Xhosa initiation schools are set up in rural areas, but it has become common to find temporary lodges, erected to protect initiates from the elements, in more urban surroundings, for instance along the N2 motorway linking Cape Town to the airport. The structures include materials obtained from dealers who specialise in supplying the inhabitants of informal urban settlements with cardboard packaging and outdated magazine posters to insulate their homes. These shelters are burnt at the end of the period of seclusion (*opposite*).

La plupart des écoles d'initiations xhosas sont établies dans les campagnes, mais il est devenu courant de voir des écoles provisoires dans les zones urbaines, comme au long de l'autoroute N2 qui relie Cape Town à l'aéroport. Ces constructions sont faites de

matériaux de récupération, obtenus de marchands qui se spécialisent dans la fourniture de vieux cartons et de papiers aux habitants des bidonvilles bordant les faubourgs. Ces abris sont brûlés au terme de la période d'isolement (*ci-dessus*).

Meistens werden Initiationslager der Xhosa in abgelegenen Landgebieten errichtet, aber mittlerweile findet man solche zeitweiligen Unterkünfte, um die Initianden vor den Elementen zu schützen, auch in Stadtgebieten, wie entlang der N2 Autobahn, auf dem Wege von Kapstadt zum Flughafen. Die Materialien dazu beschaffen sie sich von Händlern, die darauf spezialisiert sind, die Einwohner von ‚Wilden Siedlungen' mit Packpappe und alten Postern zu beliefern, um ihre Behausungen abzudichten. Die Unterkünfte werden nach Ablauf der Schulung verbrannt (*oben*).

At the end of the initiation period, young men wash to remove the clay covering their bodies. In some cases, they also smear their bodies with oil before wrapping themselves in new blankets, underlining the fact that they have left the past behind them.

A la fin de la période d'initiation, les jeunes gens se lavent de la couche d'argile qui les recouvre. Dans certaines circonstances ils s'enduisent aussi d'huile avant de se revêtir d'une nouvelle couverture, marquant ainsi qu'ils sont passés à l'étape suivante.

Am Ende der Initiationszeit waschen sich die jungen Männer den Lehm von den Körpern. Manchmal reiben sie sich auch mit Öl ein, ehe sie sich in neue Decken hüllen und damit versinnbildlichen, daß sie die Vergangenheit hinter sich gelassen haben.

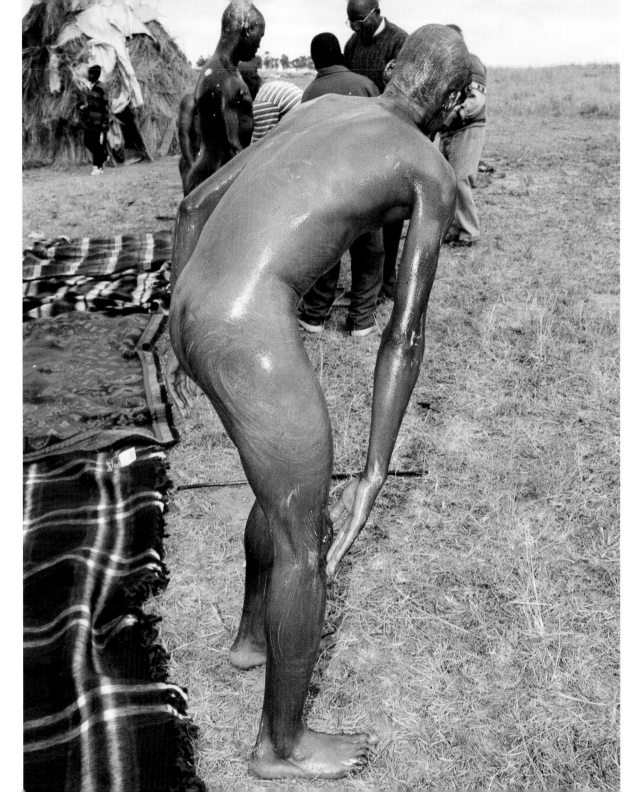

Just before the initiation lodge is set alight, Xhosa initiates turn away without looking back, signalling that their responsibilities are to the future, and to the realities of adult life. In most cases, this includes taking care, financially and otherwise, of the family.

Avant que l'école d'initiation ne soit mise à feu, les Xhosas lui tournent le dos, indiquant ainsi qu'ils acceptent les responsabilités et les réalités de la vie adulte. Ce qui, dans la plupart des cas, signifie de s'occuper des besoins, financiers ou autres, de la famille.

Unmittelbar vor Anzünden des Initiationsslagers, drehen sich Xhosa-Initianden um. Sie wenden sich der Zukunft zu und stellen sich den Verantwortungen eines Erwachsenen. In den meisten Fällen bedeutet dies die Unterstützung der Familie, finanziell und anders.

In the mid-1980s Zulu King Goodwill Zwelethini introduced a Reed Ceremony similar to that held annually in Swaziland, the previous home of his first wife. Although the primary purpose of this event is to celebrate the fertility of young women, it also affords an opportunity to encourage them to refrain from indulging in premarital sexual relations.

Vers le milieu des années 80, le roi des Zoulous, Goodwill Zwelethini, introduisit une 'Reed Ceremony' (cérémonie des roseaux) semblable à celle du Swaziland, pays d'origine de sa première épouse. Bien que la principale raison d'être de cet événement soit de fêter la fécondité des jeunes femmes, c'est aussi l'occasion de les encourager à s'abstenir d'avoir des relations sexuelles avant le mariage.

Mitte der achtziger Jahre führte König Goodwill Zwelethini die ‚Schilfzeremonie' ein, wie sie alljährlich in Swasiland, der Heimat seiner ersten Frau, abgehalten wird. Obwohl der Grundgedanke dieser Zeremonie das Feiern der Fruchtbarkeit junger Frauen ist, bietet es auch die Gelegenheit, sie zu ermahnen, keinen vorehelichen Geschlechtsverkehr zu haben.

Some Zulu-speaking families still organise coming-out ceremonies for their daughters. Money pinned to the young women's hair by guests is used to buy their dowry. They wear a caul of fat from an ox (*opposite*). These cauls symbolise the protection of the ancestors, who are responsible for ensuring the well-being and fertility of all their descendants.

Il y a encore des familles zouloues qui fêtent les débuts de leurs filles. L'argent attaché dans les cheveux des jeunes femmes par les invités sera utilisé pour leur dot. Elles portent une coiffe de graisse de bœuf (*ci-contre*). Ces coiffes représentent la protection reçue des ancêtres responsables du bien-être et de la fécondité de toutes leurs descendantes.

Manche Zulufamilien veranstalten noch eine Einführungszeremonie für ihre Töchter. Geld, das Gäste der jungen Frau an den Haaren festklammern, wird für die Aussteuer verwendet. Die junge Frau trägt eine Haube aus Ochsenfett (*gegenüber*), welche den Schutz der Ahnen symbolisiert, die für das Wohlergehen und die Fruchtbarkeit all ihrer Nachfahren zuständig sind.

In the Drakensberg region of KwaZulu-Natal, young women participate in communal coming-out ceremonies, during which they wear similar garments and perform a series of intricate movements. The gifts they receive include portable radios or CD-players.

Au KwaZulu-Natal, dans la région du Drakensberg, les jeunes débutantes portent des vêtements semblables et font une danse aux pas compliqués. Parmi les présents qu'elles reçoivent se trouvent des radios portatives ou des lecteurs CD.

Im Gebiet der Drakensberge in KwaZulu-Natal nehmen junge Frauen an gemeinschaftlichen Einführungszeremonien teil, wo sie einheitlich gekleidet sind und komplizierte Bewegungen vorführen. Zu ihren Geschenken zählen CD-Spieler und tragbare Radios.

Bantwane grooms frequently wear a suit and tie while the bride appears in traditional dress. These rural weddings involve displays of gifts that the bride gives to the groom and his parents, and the consumption of huge quantities of home-brewed beer and meat.

Les jeunes mariés bantwanes s'habillent souvent en costume cravate, alors que la mariée porte l'accoutrement traditionnel. A ces noces rurales on expose les cadeaux que la mariée fait à son époux et ses parents; on y consomme aussi d'énormes quantités de bière-maison et de viandes.

Der Bräutigam trägt bei den Bantwane oft Anzug und Krawatte, während die Braut in Volkstracht erscheint. Bei diesen ländlichen Hochzeiten werden die Geschenke der Braut an die Schwiegerfamilie ausgestellt und riesige Mengen Fleisch und Bier verkonsumiert.

The wedding ceremonies of Swazi and Zulu traditionalists involve elaborate rituals aimed at ensuring the future co-operation of the ancestors of the bride and groom. Among them is the practice of slaughtering an ox and attaching gall bladders to the bride's head. The presentation of symbolically important gifts, such as sleeping mats, to the groom's family is also central to these events.

Les noces des traditionalistes swazis et zoulous comprennent des rites compliqués dont le but est d'obtenir la collaboration des ancêtres du jeune couple. Il y a entre autres la coutume de sacrifier un bœuf et d'attacher des vésicules biliaires de chèvres sur la tête de la mariée, ainsi que l'offrande d'importants présents symboliques à la famille du jeune marié, tels que des nattes.

Hochzeitszeremonien der Swasi und Zulu beinhalten umfangreiche Rituale, die auf zukünftige Zusammenarbeit zwischen den Ahnen der Braut und denen des Bräutigams abzielen. Unter anderem wird ein Ochse geschlachtet und eine Gallenblase am Kopf der Braut befestigt. Das Überreichen symbolisch bedeutsamer Geschenke, wie Schlafmatten, an die Familie des Bräutigams ist wesentlicher Bestandteil dieser Feiern.

In present-day KwaZulu-Natal, the gifts brides bring with them to their new homes may include kists decorated with Christian icons and the money they receive from guests attending their weddings (*left*). Gifts from the bride's family are off-set by *ilobolo* payments to her father. Traditionally, these payments were made in cattle.

Les présents que les jeunes mariées du KwaZulu-Natal apportent à leur nouvelle maison comprennent des coffres décorés de symboles chrétiens, ainsi que l'argent reçu des invités aux noces (*à gauche*). Les cadeaux offerts par la famille de la mariée compensent pour les payements reçus par son père pour l'*ilobolo*. Traditionnellement ces payements consistaient en têtes de bétail.

Im heutigen KwaZulu-Natal schließen die Gaben, die eine Braut in ihr neues Heim mitbringt, auch mit christlichen Ikonen verzierte Truhen ein und Geld, das ihr von Hochzeitsgästen überreicht wurde (*links*). Geschenke der Brautfamilie werden durch die *ilobolo* Zahlungen an ihren Vater ausgeglichen. Traditionsgemäß wurden diese Zahlungen in Form von Rindern geleistet.

Today, the weddings of important leaders like Zulu King Goodwill Zwelethini generally include two ceremonies: one traditional and the other Christian. In many rural communities people who attend church services also practise rituals aimed at appeasing their ancestors, and consequently this integration of different belief systems is widely accepted.

De nos jours les noces de chefs importants comme le roi zoulou Goodwill Zweletini, comprennent généralement 2 cérémonies: une traditionnelle, et l'autre chrétienne. Dans les campagnes, les gens qui vont aux offices religieux pratiquent aussi les rituels destinés à apaiser leurs ancêtres; en conséquence l'assimilation de ces croyances très différentes est généralement bien reçue.

Heutzutage schließen Hochzeiten von wichtigen Führern, wie König Goodwill Zwelethini, gewöhnlich zwei Zeremonien ein: die traditionelle und die christliche. In vielen ländlichen Gemeinden begehen Bewohner, die ein kirchliches Zeremoniell haben, auch Rituale zur Beschwichtigung der Ahnen. Dementsprechend ist diese Integration der unterschiedlichen Glauben weit verbreitet.

When Zindzi, the youngest daughter of former President Mandela, married she wore Masai and other beadwork with an outfit based on Xhosa traditional dress. This attests to the growing importance contemporary South Africans attach to their African heritage.

Quand l'une des filles de l'ancien président Mandela se maria, sa robe était inspirée du costume traditionnel des Xhosas; elle avait aussi des ornements en perles masais. Ceci témoigne de l'importance grandissante que les Sud Africains donnent à leur patrimoine africain.

Als eine der Töchter von Altpräsident Mandela heiratete, trug sie Perlenschmuck der Masai und anderer Völker zu einem Kleid, das der Tracht der Xhosa angeglichen war. Es zeigt die zunehmende Bedeutung, die Südafrikaner ihrem afrikanischen Erbe beimessen.

Like other communities in South Africa, Sotho speakers in the Free State often combine Christian religious services with rituals aimed at appeasing their ancestors (*right bottom*). At these ceremonies people wear hybrid forms of dress that include the blankets commonly associated with South Sotho traditionalists and various types of cloths, some decorated with brightly coloured braidwork panels.

Comme d'autres communautés sud-africaines, les Sothos du Free State souvent combinent les offices chrétiens avec les rituels destinés à apaiser les ancêtres (*à droite en bas*). Lors de ces cérémonies, les participants portent des accoutrements disparates comprenant la couverture traditionnelle des Sothos, avec diverses sortes d'étoffes, certaines ornées de sections tressées aux couleurs vives.

Genau wie andere Volksgruppen in Südafrika, verbinden sotho-sprachige Christen im Freistaat oft christliche Gottesdienste mit Ritualen, die an die Ahnen gerichtet sind (*rechts*). Zu diesen Feierlichkeiten werden auch Kleidungsstücke kombiniert, wie etwa die traditionellen Decken der Süd-Sotho mit verschiedenen Stoffarten, manche mit farbenfreudigen Borten verziert.

While many rural traditionalists practise Christianity, they still rely on healers and ritual specialists to mediate between them and the ancestors. At the initiation of these mediators the powers of the ancestors are invoked by dancing and covering the face in clay.

De nombreux traditionalistes son chrétiens, mais ils dépendent toujours des spécialistes rituels qui servent de médiateurs avec les ancêtres. A l'initiation de ces médiateurs, la puissance ancestrale est invoquée par la danse et l'application d'argile sur le visage.

Zwar sind viele ländliche Traditionalisten Christen, aber sie verlassen sich dennoch auf Heilkundige und Ritualisten, um zwischen ihnen und den Ahnen zu vermitteln. Die Macht der Ahnen wird herbeigerufen durch Tänze und Einschmieren der Gesichter mit Lehm.

At their initiation ceremonies, novice ritual specialists consume gall from ritually slaughtered goats. A chicken is also commonly placed on the head of a prospective candidate before being slaughtered. The initiate is then covered in the chicken's blood.

Lors des cérémonies d'initiation, les futurs spécialistes en rituels avalent le fiel d'une chèvre sacrifiée. Il est aussi coutumier de placer sur la tête du novice un poulet vivant, qui sera alors sacrifié, baignant l'initié de son sang.

Bei ihren Einführungszeremonien schlürfen Novizinnen die Galle rituell geschlachteter Ziegen. Oft wird auch ein Huhn der Kandidatin auf den Kopf gesetzt, ehe es dann geschlachtet wird, und anschließend wird sie mit dem Blut des Huhns bespritzt.

The initiation of ritual specialists includes the slaughter of goats and chickens. The goats' gall bladders are attached to initiates, who are smeared with blood. The wearing of black, red and white garments is believed to invoke the powers of the ancestors.

L'initiation des spécialistes des rituels comprend le sacrifice de chèvres et de poulets. La vésicule biliaire de la chèvre est attachée à l'initié, le barbouillant de sang. Les couleurs noires, rouges et blanches ont le pouvoir d'invoquer la puissance des ancêtres.

Zur Einführungszeremonie der Ritualisten gehört das Schlachten von Ziegen und Hühnern. Die Gallenblase der Ziegen wird an den Teilnehmern befestigt, die mit Blut bespritzt werden. Kleidung in Schwarz, Weiß und Rot soll die Macht der Ahnen herbeirufen.

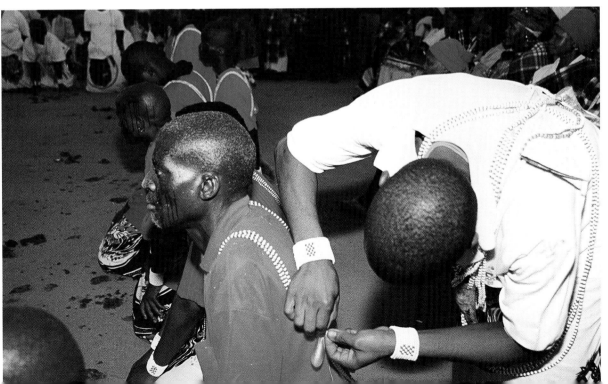

Novice initiates are expected to consume the contents from the stomachs of ritually slaughtered animals before they re-enter the community as fully fledged mediators and healers. Although in many cases initiates merely lick these bitter substances (*opposite*), they generally do eat the roasted meat obtained from these animals at the end of the initiation period.

Avant de pouvoir réintégrer leur communauté en tant que médiateurs et guérisseurs à part entière, les initiés devront consommer le contenu de l'estomac des animaux sacrifiés. Dans de nombreux cas, ils ne font que lécher ces substances amères (*ci-contre*), et souvent ils mangeront la viande rôtie de ces animaux à la fin de la période d'initiation.

Die Novizen sollten den Mageninhalt der rituell geschlachteten Tiere verzehren, bevor sie als vollwertige Vermittler und Heilkundige wieder in die Gemeinschaft aufgenommen werden. Obwohl in vielen Fällen die Teilnehmer an diesen bitteren Substanzen nur lecken (*gegenüber*), verzehren sie im allgemeinen schon das geröstete Fleisch dieser Tiere am Ende der Einführungsperiode.

Ritual specialists, who wear white, black and red beads to signify the presence of the ancestors, play a crucial role in mediating between the living and the dead. In most cases, they communicate the needs of the ancestors to their clients, thus securing the ancestors' ongoing commitment to ensuring the well-being of the living.

Les spécialistes en rituels, qui portent des perles blanches, rouges et noires indiquant la présence des ancêtres, jouent un rôle essentiel de médiateur entre les vivants et les morts. Dans la majorité des cas, ils communiquent les désirs des ancêtres à leurs descendants, obtenant la promesse que le bien-être continuel de ceux-ci sera garanti.

Ritualisten, die weiße, schwarze und rote Perlen tragen, um Anwesenheit der Ahnen zu bekunden, spielen eine entscheidende Vermittlerrolle zwischen Lebenden und Toten. Meistens übermitteln sie Forderungen der Ahnen an deren Nachfahren, um damit zu versichern, daß die Ahnen sich weiterhin um das Wohlergehen der lebenden Familienmitglieder kümmern.

Throughout rural South Africa, important ceremonies like weddings and various kinds of initiation almost invariably culminate in celebrations aimed at praising and thanking the ancestors. In most cases, these celebrations are accompanied by dance sequences, most of which are orchestrated with the assistance of musical instruments, including carved drums and plastic whistles.

Dans toutes les campagnes sud africaines, les cérémonies importantes telles que les noces et diverses formes d'initiation, se terminent presque toujours en remerciant et rendant hommage aux ancêtres. Dans la majorité des cas, ces célébrations comprennent des danses, dont la plupart sont accompagnées avec des instruments de musique, comme ces tambours ornés de sculptures et des sifflets en plastique.

In allen Landgebieten Südafrikas klingen wichtige Zeremonien, wie Hochzeiten und die unterschiedlichen Einführungen, fast immer in Feierlichkeiten aus, die mit Lobpreisungen und Dankesbezeigungen den Ahnen gewidmet sind. Diese Feierlichkeiten gehen oft mit Tänzen einher, die mehrheitlich von Instrumenten wie geschnitzten Trommeln und Plastikflöten musikalisch begleitet werden.

Drums used during ceremonies by independent church groups are generally based on drums of European origin, that were first introduced to South Africa by British military bands. But there are also other drums, now less commonly used, that are based on the African model of stretching a membrane over only one end of a hollow wooden vessel.

Les tambours utilisés au cours des offices religieux indépendants, sont généralement basés sur les tambours européens, qui furent introduits en Afrique du Sud par les fanfares militaires britanniques. Mais il y a aussi d'autres tambours, plus rares, basés sur le style africain où une seule membrane est tendue à l'une des extrémités de l'instrument.

Trommeln, die bei Festlichkeiten der unabhängigen Kirchen verwendet werden, gleichen gewöhnlich jenen aus Europa, wie sie einst von britischen Militärkapellen in Südafrika eingeführt wurden. Aber es gibt auch andere Trommeln, heutzutage weniger verwandt, wobei nach afrikanischer Art nur eine Öffnung des Holzinstruments mit Haut bespannt wird.

Some bugles played at ceremonies and rites of passage are made from animal horns, and are generally played by women. But it is quite common to find people with old trumpets and other Western instruments participating in some of these events.

Certains des clairons utilisés lors des cérémonies et des rites de passage sont fait de la corne d'un animal, et joués généralement par des femmes. Les gens participent couramment à ces événements avec des vieilles trompettes et autres instruments occidentaux.

Einige der Hörner, die bei festlichen Anlässen und ‚Riten des Übergangs' gespielt werden, sind aus Tiergeweihen und werden normalerweise von Frauen gespielt. Aber häufig findet man auch Teilnehmer mit alten Trompeten und anderen westlichen Instrumenten.

Competitive displays of dancing often take place at coming-out and other ceremonies. Dancers demonstrating their skills are encouraged by onlookers, who generally provide the necessary musical accompaniment. Today, dancers also perform for tourists.

Les cérémonies et festivités comprennent souvent des concours de danse où les spectateurs eux-même fournissent parfois l'accompagnement musical. De nos jours, les danseurs donnent également des représentations pour les touristes.

Tanzwettbewerbe finden oft bei Einführungs- und anderen Feierlichkeiten statt. Tänzer, die ihr Talent vorführen, werden von Zuschauern angefeuert, die meist auch die musikalische Untermalung liefern. Heutzutage gibt es auch Tanzvorführungen für Touristen.

In most South African communities dancing is a form of celebration and worship, and garments are designed to accentuate the movement of the dancers. In the case of beadwork and clothing worn by Tsonga dancers, colour highlights their movements.

La danse est une forme de célébration et un acte de dévotion; les costumes sont conçus pour accentuer les mouvements. Dans le cas des danseurs tsongas, ce sont les couleurs de leurs costumes et des ornements de perles qui soulignent les mouvements.

Bei den meisten Volksgruppen Südafrikas ist Tanz ein Ausdruck des Feierns und der Anbetung, und die Kleidung unterstreicht die Bewegungen der Tänzer. Bei den Tsonga lenken auch Farben und Perlenschmuck die Aufmerksamkeit auf die Bewegungen.